Narcissistic Abuse Recovery

A Self Healing Emotional Guide Through the Stages of Recovery from Emotionally Abusive Relationships with a Narcissist

By: Alison Care

© Copyright 2019 by Alison Care - All rights reserved.

This content is provided with the sole purpose of providing relevant information on a specific topic for which every reasonable effort has been made to ensure that it is both accurate and reasonable. Nevertheless, by purchasing this content you consent to the fact that the author, as well as the publisher, are in no way experts on the topics contained herein, regardless of any claims as such that may be made within. As such, any suggestions or recommendations that are made within are done so purely for entertainment value. It is recommended that you always consult a professional prior to undertaking any of the advice or techniques discussed within.

This is a legally binding declaration that is considered both valid and fair by both the Committee of Publishers Association and the American Bar Association and should be considered as legally binding within the United States.

The reproduction, transmission, and duplication of any of the content found herein, including any specific or extended information will be done as an illegal act regardless of the end from the information ultimately takes. This includes copied versions of the work both physical, digital and audio unless express consent of the Publisher is provided beforehand. Any additional rights reserved.

Furthermore, the information that can be found within the pages described forthwith shall be considered both accurate and truthful when it comes to the recounting of facts. As such, any use, correct or incorrect, of the provided information will render the Publisher free of responsibility as to the actions taken outside of their direct purview. Regardless, there are zero scenarios where the original author or the Publisher can be deemed liable in any fashion for any damages or hardships that may result from any of the information discussed herein.

Additionally, the information in the following pages is intended only for informational purposes and should thus be thought of as universal. As befitting its nature, it is presented without assurance regarding its prolonged validity or interim quality. Trademarks that are mentioned are done without written consent and can in no way be considered an endorsement from the trademark holder.

ISBN: 9781074162726

Table of Contents

Introduction 6

Chapter 1: Basics of Narcissistic Abuse 9

Chapter 2: Types of Narcissistic Abuse 31

    Outbursts: The Narcissist's Reaction to Shame 44

    Gas Lighting: How the Narcissist Distorts Their and Your Reality ... 45

    Boundary Violation: The Narcissist Neither Understands nor Respects Them 47

    Reciprocation: The Narcissist Does Not Reciprocate 48

Chapter 3: Acknowledging Abuse and Setting Your Intention Toward Recovery 50

    Your Reaction to Shame After Narcissistic Abuse 61

    Your New Tendency to Distort Reality 64

    Your New Difficulty With Boundaries 65

    Your New Difficulty to Reciprocate 67

Chapter 4: Recommended Activities for Recovery . 72

    Going on Walks 75

    Playing With Yoga Poses 80

Chapter 5: Recommended Activities for Reclaiming Your Identity 89

Interviewing Yourself 90

Reinvigorating Your Sense Perceptions................................ 96

Therapy.. 99

Chapter 6: Recommended Activities for Regaining Control 103

Interacting With Pets... 103

Gardening 108

Chapter 7: Practicing Daily Affirmation................ 115

You Are Good Enough 116

You Deserve to be Happy 118

It is Okay to Feel Shame Sometimes 119

Love Yourself for Loving Others (Even Narcissists) 120

Be Proud of What You Learned from Your Experience 121

Be Proud of Who You Have Become 122

Be Proud of Your Boundaries.. 123

Be Proud of Your Ability to Feel Shame 124

Be Proud of Your Desire to Know Reality Over Fantasy................ 125

Be Proud of Who You Are 126

You Deserve to Recover.. 127

You Deserve a Better Relationship 129

Chapter 8: Allowing Yourself to Be Who You Are 130

Separate Your Identity from the Narcissist 131

Find Something That Makes You Feel Strong 133

Be Extremely Honest and Upfront 134

Be Assertive 136
Be Outgoing 137
Try New Things..138
Do Volunteer Work 140
Be Humble, but Don't Minimize Your Accomplishments..............142
Seek Counsel from Others 143
Take Yourself to Dinner 145
Keep a Record of Your Work...146

Conclusion 148

Introduction

Congratulations on purchasing *Narcissistic Abuse Recovery: How to Recover Emotionally from a Relationship with a Narcissist and Reclaim Your Identity,* and thank you for doing so.

The following chapters will discuss a two-fold topic. The first four chapters will discuss what narcissistic abuse is and the different forms it takes on. The first chapter will go over the basics.

The second chapter will discuss the types of narcissist that exist. The third chapter will explain the importance of acknowledging the type of abuse suffered and how to set an intention toward recovery.

The fourth chapter will get you started getting active about your recovery. It will provide you activities that will reinvigorate your senses, which will eventually link you back to your sense of self in particular.

The fifth chapter provides more activities specifically meant to promote a healthy sense of self in order to reclaim your identity.

The sixth chapter offers an activity that will help you practice regaining control in your life, starting with your own body.

The seventh chapter focuses on the general activity of affirming yourself and stresses the importance of practicing these affirmations daily.

The eighth chapter discusses the path to allowing yourself to become yourself again with your rejuvenated identity and reclamation of strength and control.

This book does not blame the victim or offer its readers the secret to dealing with, living with, or being with someone with Narcissistic Personality Disorder. This document is about recovery from the emotional abuse of which someone with Narcissistic Personality Disorder is capable.

There are plenty of books on this subject on the market, thanks again for choosing this one! Every effort was made to ensure it is full of as much useful information as possible. Please enjoy!

Chapter 1: Basics of Narcissistic Abuse

Narcissistic Personality Disorder is, like most disorders, a spectrum. A lot of people fall on this spectrum without ever being diagnosed or facing any major issues in their lives or relationships. Others face the consequences for their behavior, and those who form relationships with them become victims of narcissistic abuse.

If you're reading this book, you probably already know something about narcissistic personality disorder and what it is like to be in a relationship with someone on that particular spectrum. Let's briefly discuss the kind of abuse someone with Narcissistic Personality has a tendency to do, either intentionally or unintentionally.

Did the person you are trying to recover from making you feel as though you could never be good enough?

This is a result of narcissistic abuse. A narcissist makes the person they are with feel this way because that's the way they feel. They don't think anyone who is not them is good enough. The part-worth thinking is about the most with regard to this feeling is what it means about your sense of self. The fact that they have made you feel like you could never be good enough for them does not necessarily have to be a problem in and of itself.

Not being good enough for them does not have to mean you are not good enough for yourself or anyone else. You give them power when you make the logical leap from feeling not good enough for them to feeling not good enough for anyone. Don't be too hard on yourself to make this logical leap. The narcissist you were with probably pushed you to make it. It is easy to feel worthless after any kind of rejection. Human beings often make a single mistake and feel as though they are completely incompetent as a result. Try to back up and see the matter for what it is. Not being good enough for a narcissist has nothing to do with how good you are. What makes them a narcissist is the fact that no one else will ever be good enough for them. To move toward your recovery, you need to start measuring yourself by some other standard than the one the narcissist you were withheld you to.

Did the person you are trying to recover from making you feel as though you were undeserving of them or anyone else?

This is a result of narcissistic abuse. This is probably what helped you make that leap in logic to feeling that, if you did not deserve the love of the narcissist, you had put so much of your time and love towards, you did not deserve love at all. This is still problematic thinking.

If the narcissist made you feel as though you did not deserve them or anyone else of their caliber, they were pushing you to determine that measuring up to them and their standards are the only way to be measured. Once they could convince you of this, your self-worth became more up to them than it was to you. Or, at least they had you believing such a thing. You're going to need to stop believing the lies that they had you believing. You're going to need to stop seeing yourself through their eyes. You need to reclaim your identity so that you can evaluate yourself.

When they made you feel as though you did not deserve them, they made you want to deserve them. Then, all of your work became all about them. Everything you did become about deserving them. That was never the point for the narcissist. You were never going to get to a point where you would finally deserve them. The point was always for them to make you feel as if deserving them was your life's work. This simply is not what your life's work is, unless your name is Sisyphus and the Greek gods have punished you to an eternity of pushing a boulder up a hill only to let it fall back down to the ground and start pushing it up again.

There is no real work to be done when it comes to deserving a narcissist. A narcissist deserves only himself or herself for as long as a narcissist only wants to be with him or herself. It is not your job to make them change. And, if it were, you would not be helping by trying to win their approval. You'd only been exacerbated their condition.

Did the person you are trying to recover from constant need affirmation, but never seemed to affirm you in anything?

This is a result of narcissistic abuse. Narcissists need constant affirmation, but they don't really care if other people need it too. They will give it when it gets them something. They like to affirm the people who have the things they want the most. They will gladly affirm the people who look the way they want to look or have the things they want to have. It is unlikely that this is the kind of affirmation you were looking for in your relationship.

You might have felt at times that you weren't good enough for the narcissist you were with because, though they praised others frequently, they never praised you. This probably made you feel unworthy of praise. This probably also had you convinced that this wasn't the narcissist's fault, but rather your own.

It was not your fault. It wasn't even a fault in your logic, really. Your logic was that if the narcissist you were with were incapable of giving praise, you would not hear them praising others either. Yet, you did hear them praising others often. So, you thought you might get praise if you deserved it like the others. But it never came, did it? Or, if it did, it was only because you did something for the narcissist, it wasn't because you did something for yourself or your self-improvement. The reason for this is because the narcissist does not care what you do for yourself. A narcissist only cares what you do for them or what you could do for them.

When a narcissist is praising others in front of you (which, of course, you find hurtful because you are starving for such praise for yourself), it is because at a distance, they praise what they want. If you get something they want and tangle it in front of them, they are either going to flatter you into getting it from you or shame you from having it. Narcissists are resentful.

They will praise the watch of another woman or man, but if you end up buying that watch for yourself, it will not impress them. They wanted you to buy that watch for them. They wanted to have it. They did not want you to have it. You may have thought that getting the thing they praised on another would make you more deserving of them, but that is not the case. The reason for this has already been discussed. Deserving them was never really on the table. It only mattered to them that you always *believed* you did not deserve them.

It is time to stop believing such nonsense. You deserve to measure yourself with your own meter. You deserve to enjoy the things that you have without worrying that having them is upsetting your covetous lover. You deserve to feel good about your accomplishments without believing that their lack of praise means anything about their merit. You deserve to stop thinking desserts were ever a real aspect of your relationship with a narcissist.

Did the person you are trying to recover from seem to think they deserved a life far better than the one they had, which made you feel as though they believed they would have been better off without you?

This is another result of narcissistic abuse. Another aspect of Narcissistic Personality Disorder is entitlement. Narcissists believe they are entitled to wealth, riches, and glamour without having to work for any of it. It is always someone else's fault that they do not have what they wish they had. Since you were their partner, it is likely that they often made you feel like their bad luck in life was your fault, or if they could not quite manage that, they made you feel bad that you had a better lot in life than they did.

According to the narcissist, you were leading the life you deserved or one better than you deserved; however, they were leading a life less than they thought they deserved. These probably made you feel like either you were unable to give them the life they deserved or their next form of punishment in their unlucky lot in life.

Again, this is a myth they told you over and over. You don't need to believe it anymore. You can make up your own mind about what you deserve or does not deserve.

You don't have to believe that they deserved better than you.

You don't have to believe that you don't deserve better than them. You get to choose how you think life's hardships are dealt with. You don't have to listen to the narcissist anymore. You can make up your mind about your lot and theirs. You can change your mind about whatever it is that the narcissist made you think. You can decide for yourself what you think you deserve or do not deserve. Perhaps, you don't think anyone deserves anything, that's fine. This book is not meant to tell you whether or not the narcissist who you were with deserved or didn't deserve you. The point is that they had no right to tell you such things either, so stop listening to them.

Did the person you are trying to recover from often seem stuck in the world of fantasies, so the reality was never good enough?

This is a result of narcissistic abuse. Each aspect of their personality disorder pushed you to determine that you could not make them happy. It might be true that you could not but it was not because you did not do enough. You might have done more than enough. It's just that a narcissist can never get enough from the real world because a narcissist lives in the mythic world they created for themselves where they are the most important thing. They will do their best to pull anyone who will let them into that myth. You may have lived with that myth with them. They probably made you feel at times like they were more important than you or anyone else. This was not true then. This is not true now.

Yet, for as long as it seemed true, you were comparing yourself to a fantasy world that you could never really exist. You could help the narcissist with their own feeling that they were more important than others, but you could not really be part of their fantasy, nor could you meet the requirements of their mythic expectations. You were never going to be able to turn your reality into their fantasy because you belong to this reality. The expectations for you to do so were nonsensical and, perhaps, cruel. It may not have been cruel in the sense that the narcissist knew what they were doing, but it was cruel in the sense that you were once again asked to do the impossible. You were never going to be able to make their life what they wished it to be because what they wished for was a fantasy. You were not reaching for reasonable goals. You were striving to be a fairytale. That was never going to happen. Now, it is time for you to make sure you never fall victim to the same disorder. You have to embrace reality now if you want to recover.

Did the person you are trying to recover from was obsess over the image as if it was the most important thing in the world and make you believe you should feel the same way about that?

This is a result of narcissistic abuse. Image is, simply, not everything, even if it is a lot, because the image is an important part of the civilization and the way human beings understand themselves and the world around them, it is not very hard for a narcissist to convince others that image matters more than anything. In truth, image matters. The false part is that it is not the only thing that matters. Believing it is the only thing that matters is the root of narcissism. They are the way they are because their own sense of self is empty, so they try to fill it (unsuccessfully) with the praise and affirmation of others.

They will discourage you from carrying your own substantial sense of self with you. It is another thing that they are jealous of you for having because they don't. They will make you feel bad for having this thing that they don't, but they won't describe it as such. They will make you feel bad for caring more about something other than the image. They will make your expression of a substantive thought or feeling seem insignificant by comparison to an image. This may have happened to you. It may have made you feel that the more you expressed your identity, the more your narcissistic partner pushed you away. This is because they were uncomfortable with you having your own identity because it meant that you were not dependent upon their approval for your sense of self-worth. The way they are dependent upon everyone's approval for their sense of self-worth.

You don't have to live like that anymore. Now, you can embrace your own sense of self. If you were unable to make things work with a narcissist, it probably means that you have your own identity, and the narcissist eventually could not keep you around for their own needs. Your recovery will mean getting to know yourself again and being happy to do so. You should learn to feel good about expressing yourself in ways you would not have done in front of the narcissist you were with.

You should find people who seem to appreciate your expressions of depth and self-assuredness, find people who appreciate what is beneath the surface. Also, spend time with those who care about more than aesthetics. You should be with people who search for meaning in and beyond an image. You should be with people who appreciate that you do the same.

Did the person you are trying to recover from making you feel worthless because you could not make them see your worth?

This is a result of narcissistic abuse. A narcissist has a way of meddling in basic logic. It is not the case that you are worthless because someone does not recognize your worth, but a narcissist can, certainly, help you form this kind of false conclusion. You have to start seeing your worth differently. Being with a narcissist has a way of making you attach your worth to what they see, but your recovery will require that you put a distance between your worth and what they see. What they see isn't about you anyway; it's about them. It's always about them. That's what their disorder means. Since it isn't about you, it does not make sense to attach your worth to them because they aren't good judges.

Yet, they are good at making others feel worthless. The reason they like to do this is because it makes them feel as though they are worth more than they are. They feel worthless often because they have no true sense of who they are. All they know about themselves is that they are more important than anyone else and that they deserve more than they have. So, making others feel worthless, makes them feel more important than others.

It also makes them feel better about not having more than they have when they make the people they are jealous of feeling worthless. This is an expression of their resentment. When they are jealous of someone who has something they don't have, their response is to try to find a way to make sure that person can't enjoy whatever it is they have. If you have a nice new watch that they wish they had, they'll say something negative about the watch so that you can't enjoy it as much anymore.

By making you feel your watch is worthless, they feel better about not having it. It is an empty path, but it is how a narcissist operates. They do it this way because all that matters to them are feeling more important than others making them feel as though they are less important helps them accomplish their goal.

It has to stop somewhere. You can put a stop to it with you. Once you stop letting narcissist mess with your logical abilities, you can get to a point where you don't let their evaluations become your evaluations. You can do this retroactively with certain items. Keeping with the example of a narcissist coveting a watch and then saying something negative about it, it would be good for someone in recovery to find that watch and start wearing it again.

The point is simply to decide for yourself how you feel about something that the narcissist you were with did not like. You might find that, from a distance, you remember that you actually quite liked something that a narcissist convinced you was deplorable. This kind of activity is a step toward recovery, reclaiming your identity, and regaining your control.

Did it shock you to discover by the end of your relationship that despite the amount of time you were together, they still did not seem to really know you?

This is a result of narcissistic abuse. Because someone with Narcissistic Personality Disorder thinks images and aesthetics are more important than anything else, a narcissist never really gets to know anyone in depth. If they do, it is because they are obsessed with a person's image. The depth may come along with that image, but it isn't really important for a narcissist.

The narcissist may have shown an interest in something about you when they needed something from you, but they did not really care to maintain that knowledge. They just needed to know it to get something at the time. Once they got it, they forgot whatever they have learned about you because it wasn't really important to them.

Narcissists get to know other people the way bad students study for tests. They just memorize what they think is going to be on the test. They have no interest in actually learning anything. They want the grade, but they don't feel they need the knowledge. When a narcissist wants something, they can do what it takes to get that thing.

This does not mean they will care to remember it. Just like a bad student will forget everything they studied because they only studied the night before a test, a narcissist will forget what they learned about a person as soon as they no longer need to know it to get what they want.

You need to accept this, though it may be painful to do so. It is not because you were not worth getting to know. It is not because you are not interesting. It is because they did not care to remember what they learned.

That is not your fault, none of this is. If we return to the analogy of the bad student studying the night before a test and forgetting everything after the test, we can see that the fault is not with the subject.

We know those bad students will do this no matter how fascinating the material is. The material might be practical knowledge about medicine. The point is not about the material. The material makes no difference. The point is that a bad student and a narcissist forget what they learned because learning it was never their goal. They were only doing what they needed to do to get something out of it—and that thing was not simply the benefit of gaining knowledge about something or someone.

Did you feel as though this person needed love, but never seemed to be able to get enough of it from you?

This is a result of narcissistic abuse. A narcissist often appears to others as if they are desperately in need of love. In a sense, it is true—they are. The grey area is that a narcissist never seems to get their fill of love. The fallacy in operation here is the jump to the conclusion that their need for love must mean they don't have enough. It is not a senseless conclusion, but it is a fallacy. When it comes to a narcissist, the need for love does not necessarily indicate a lack of love. A narcissist can have a whole lot of love and still seem to need more. Love feeds a narcissist. They are not easily satisfied. You must have felt that at some point. You probably made the thought that it was your fault that you could not satisfy them. This was worse for you to make than the previous fallacy.

It was not your fault that you could not satisfy a narcissist. Perhaps they did need more. Perhaps you did not give them enough to satisfy them. However, you cannot fault yourself for this because a narcissist needs too much and is never satisfied by others. A fairly logical conclusion to draw at this point is that you were never able to satisfy them because they were never going to be satisfied by you.

The reason for this is that they cannot be satisfied by others because they will be unhappy for as long as they are empty within themselves. They tried to empty you so that they could fill themselves, but they could not. They were unsuccessful because you are not them. They cannot fill themselves with you. They did try to drain you, however. Because of that, you will need to fill yourself back up until you feel full again.

Did it shock you to discover that, perhaps, the person you were with and gave so much love to may never have really loved you the way you tried so hard to love them?

This is perhaps a result of narcissistic abuse, but perhaps a major step toward your recovery. If, in fact, the person you were in a relationship has a Narcissistic Personality Disorder, then the incapacity to love is part of their psychological disposition. If this is the case, then they probably never really loved you the way you loved them. It is important that you recognize that the reason for this is *not* that you are unworthy of love. It is that they are incapable of it.

Understanding that they did not love you *because* they were incapable of it will help you understand that you *are* worthy of love because you *are* capable of it. You are not unworthy of love because a narcissist could not love you. They could not love you because a narcissist is incapable of loving someone other than themselves.

It is time for you to take a cue from the narcissist by loving yourself, but do not lose your capacity to love others. It is precisely your capacity to love others that makes you worthy of love.

As you recover, embrace the idea of love as reciprocity. Love can be the two-way street you wanted it to be. It just isn't that way with a narcissist. It's always a one-way with them. That is not the way you made it, it's the way they did it.

Now, you can find your way to a two-way street again. You just have to remember to love others *and* love yourself. Keep that two-way street alive within your own heart. Your recovery requires both.

Without learning to love yourself again, you won't be able to undo what the narcissist has done. Without keeping your ability to love others alive, you might become like the narcissist and find yourself as empty as they always tried to make you feel.

Love yourself. Know yourself. Reclaim your identity. Regain your control. Find a way to be comfortable being yourself again. That's what this book is about.

Chapter 2: Types of Narcissistic Abuse

As you recover, you must understand that narcissism breed narcissism. One important thing to know about the narcissist you were in a relationship is that a narcissist more than likely raised them.

This means that the narcissist you were with most likely experienced a different kind of narcissist abuse than the kind they dealt with you. There is a difference between the kind of abuse they experienced from their parent(s)/guardian(s) and the kind of abuse you experienced in your relationship with them.

This chapter will go over both kinds of abuse so that you can understand the abuse they suffered that caused their behavior toward you. You might even get a better understanding of why they were able to disguise their narcissism in the beginning better. Think about the fact that they might have been embarrassed by their mother's or father's narcissism while they were growing up.

The children of a narcissist learn to dislike the behaviors of a narcissist, but still struggle to avoid producing those same behaviors themselves. We all know how hard it is not to fall victim to the vices of our parents. Children of narcissists might be committed to avoiding the pitfalls of their parents, but that does not mean they were necessarily able to avoid them in their relationships. It might mean they were able to hide them from you at first, though.

Basically, the problem a narcissistic parent (especially a narcissistic mother) creates the personality disorder in early age and delays a child's development. Think about the basic idea of the Oedipus Complex as you have heard about it from someone's derivation of Sigmund Freud's work. Think about what you know already. Oedipus comes from Greek mythology. In Sophocles' tragedy, the myth was explained as follows.

Oedipus was born to Jocasta and Laius, the queen and king of Thebes. Laius heard from a prophet that he (Laius) was going to be murdered by his son. So, he had his son murdered by his servant. Well, specifically, he had his son's feet bound together and had a servant to take the child to the woods to die.

The servant met another servant for another king—the king of Corinth. The king of Corinth and his wife had been struggling to produce an heir to the throne. The two servants came up with an idea. Laius' servant gave the child (Oedipus) to the servant of Polybus, the King of Corinth.

Oedipus grew up a happy prince until he heard a rumor that he was not the legitimate child of parents. Seeking answers, Oedipus sought an oracle to learn the truth of his parentage. What he discovered was that he had a worse fate in store for him than the discovery of being adopted.

The oracle said that Oedipus would kill his father, marry his mother, and die in Colonus. Oedipus fled, and never returned to Corinth because he wanted to protect his mother and father from the fate he had been told belonged to him (Oedipus).

Of course, Oedipus did not manage to escape his fate. Along his journey, he was attacked by Laius and an entourage of men. Oedipus killed Laius (his father) and all but one man in the battle at a crossroads. After this event, Oedipus encountered the riddling Sphinx that had long plagued the city of Thebes. He solved the riddle, saved Thebes, and became their king. The city of Thebes married him to their widowed queen, Jocasta (Oedipus' mother). Oedipus fulfilled his fate unknowingly.

Freud uses this myth to explain some interesting aspects of human psychology. His point is not that every man wants to sleep with his mother. He did not simply misread the play as if Oedipus *intended* or *wanted* to be with his mother.

Freud understood that Oedipus never intended to kill his father or marry his mother. The fact that Oedipus never intended to do as he did (and, in fact, actively avoided it) works with Freud's understanding of the unconscious. Freud was never saying that humans actively want to kill their fathers and marry their mothers. It was always about unconscious impulses that get developed early on in our childhoods.

The basic of narcissistic abuse from parent to child is a disruption of the traditional outline of development outlined by Freud. Basically, it's important that a child first recognizes a being other than self and that this first "other" being is the being that nurtures the child.

This might not be the child's actual mother, but the idea is the nurturer and nurse of the child is the first person the child distinguishes as something other than itself. The child notices this person first because this person directly provides for the child. The child will want to form its first connection or attachment to this person.

If the mother shows an interest and a connection is made, the child will understand the difference and connection between one human being and another. The child will even want to move on from its connection with the mother once the mother starts denying the child. Denial and shame are crucial to a child developing into something other than a narcissist. A child needs to recognize that the bond felt between mother and child has limitations. It is a mother's responsibility to enforce these limitations and deny the child. If neither the mother denies the child, nor forms a true connection, the child will be delayed in this kind of development.

This is intuitively understandable, right? A child that has formed a connection with mom and then being rejected, shamed, or denied by the mother will want to form a new connection with another being. This is important. The greater sense of difference a child develops early on, the less of a chance the child has of becoming a narcissist. The child will go on, trying to form meaningful connections.

The idea, Freud tells us is that a human being will often, unconsciously, go about trying to find the kind of libidinal experience felt very early on in the connection between mother and child. This is essentially the Oedipus Complex.

It does not mean any given man wants to kill his father and marry his mother. It means that most human beings are constantly competing and striving for the affection they once felt from their earliest connection with the being we commonly identify with the word "mother"—the first provider of essential nutrients, security, and comfort.

If a child is never given this kind of experience, the complex they experience will work out a little differently from the Oedipus Complex. The reason for this is that a connection either wasn't forged or wasn't disconnected. If a mother of a child, or a main parental figure is a narcissist, this kind of disruption of development is probable.

The reason it is likely that the narcissists struggle to connect with others, so mothers might not be able to truly connect with their child the way the child wants.

Or, the narcissist only connects with the child insofar as they see the child as an extension of themselves.

Either way, the development is abnormal. If this part of the development is it, the irregularity will produce abnormal behavior in the child for potentially the rest of their lifetime.

These are very basic insights into why the narcissist you were with was the way he or/she was. What it means will take a little more explanation. The point of understanding this is not necessarily to forgive your narcissist, but rather to understand why they were the way they were, and why it wasn't your fault that they were the way they were.

If it was anyone's fault, it was most likely whoever raised them. When they missed out on that early connection with a mother-figure, they developed some of the following symptoms, most likely.

They are never really sure of themselves, even though they feel the need to constantly pretend they are. They feel the need to exaggerate each of their achievements, especially in comparison to the achievements of others. They believe they are special, however, they are so complex and struggle to be understood by anyone. They seem to require an excess of admiration. They are covetous, arrogant, entitled, and lack empathy. The reason for all of these things has to do with the person they wanted to connect with the most and yet were unable to do so.

If they could not form a true connection with their mother, they are still stuck trying to gain that connection. They are behind, and they didn't forge a connection and then start trying to find that connection in a new being who didn't shame them the way a mother does.

They are still stuck trying to find a connection without knowing what it is actually like or what the shame felt after a connection like that. They are just underdeveloped in this way. It isn't really their fault they are delayed, but their behaviors do become their responsibility after childhood all the same.

Their behaviors are, of course, related to gaining the kind of acceptance they never achieved with their mothers. They might not behave the way their mothers did. They might actively try not to be overly arrogant. They might even readily admit their faults.

It's up to you, at this point, to decide whether or not you were in a relationship with a narcissist who was overtly fulfills the perfect diagnosis of all the things mentioned above or if, perhaps, you were with a narcissist who was good at hiding it because they were embarrassed by their narcissistic parent's behavior.

In this case, you've got a complicated experience. Just decide for yourself if you suffered the kind of abuse this book describes.

If the narcissist you were with developed narcissistic traits and tendencies, regardless of how well they were hidden during portions of your relationship, then they abused you emotionally in specific ways. Mostly, they attacked your sense of identity, your sense of reality, your sense of boundaries, and your sense of reciprocity and softness. The basics of narcissistic abuse are easier to understand once you understand a narcissist's basic struggles.

The narcissist struggles with the empty feeling perpetuated since their early childhood because they were never able to feel a true connection to a parental figure, or they were not properly shamed for feeling an overabundance of affection for a parental feeling. Their feelings toward their parents affect the way they behave in relationships.

They make you question your sense of identity because they don't understand identity normally. Their own sense of identity is either bound up with their parental figure because they are still waiting to find it through their parent's affirmation or because they achieved a sense of identity in being with their parent that has yet to be disrupted.

If the narcissist you were with was too connected to their parent and you felt you could never get between such a connection, you witnessed their lack of identity through their lack of separation between themselves and their parent.

If the narcissist you were with never really was able to forge a healthy connection with a parent, you will suffer the abuse of a narcissist that has no sense of identity because he or she is still engaged in the activity of getting parental approval.

They might have sought this from you, others, or still actively sought it from their parental figures. You may have tried to give them this connection, but it never felt like enough. That would be because you were unwilling to be their sole nurturer and thereby provide for them that unique mother-child connection they've craved since they were an infant.

This is not your fault. There is no reason you should have put it upon yourself to provide maternal affection to your partner the way a mother would provide for an infant. In fact, you probably gave your partner the sense of shame they should have experienced from their mother after forming that connection, but they did not understand how to handle this kind of shame from someone they had a sexual relationship with.

The shame that mother gives a child when she starts weaning them off of breastfeeding or other methods of sustenance are specific; it tells the child they need to deny certain desires for stimulation. When an adult is denied in this way by a lover, the feeling works differently.

For a narcissist, or really for anyone, this kind of shame from a lover is hurtful. It isn't your fault that hurt them if they were seeking the kind of connection a mother gives to an infant, but the rejection they felt probably exacerbated their narcissistic impulses.

Just like the Freudian notion of the Oedipus Complex is unconscious, so too are narcissistic impulses for a narcissist. They do not always know what they are doing. They might even try not to be narcissistic because society has shamed it, but their set of desires from the person they are with cannot be so easily hidden. And so, you suffered the abuse you suffered, which we will now turn to more directly.

Outbursts: The Narcissist's Reaction to Shame

Narcissists cannot handle the shame. Either they were never conditioned to it by their parents, or they were traumatized by it at some point during their development. In any case, they really just cannot handle it the way you can. They would rather escape it by fantasizing it away. They have to re-imagine how it happened or convince someone else it happened differently.

Narcissists do not have these outbursts all the time. It isn't like the typical narcissist, is just obviously having ridiculous outbursts every time they guess wrong at a trivia question, but the random outbursts you've probably experienced are glimpses into the honest psycho of the narcissist. The narcissist cannot stand the shame. They just can't. When something happens in a social setting and you made the narcissist you were to feel the slightest amount of shame (or, rather, they shamed themselves) what follows will often be a surprising outburst.

The reason for this is their inability to deal with shame in a healthy way. If you have been with a narcissist during one of these outbursts, you are likely to have experienced a little bit of abuse from it. They probably tried to shame you instead because they simply could not handle their own.

Gas Lighting: How the Narcissist Distorts Their and Your Reality

Narcissists are prone to magical thinking or fantasy. They avoid the reality of shame by coming up with a fantasy. They avoid feeling shame by imagining it away. Perhaps the narcissist you were with had a way of convincing you that anything they did wrong was actually your fault. The reason for this is their inability to deal with shame.

They cannot handle being ashamed of themselves, so they create a new narrative. If you are readily available, they might use you for transferring their shame too. Or, they may just make it your fault, so that they don't have to feel it all themselves.

This is probably part of the abuse you felt. They suddenly distorted reality if you tried to confront them with the slightest offense they caused you. Some parts of them felt ashamed for treating you the way they did, but they could neither admit it nor deal with it. Instead, they found the answer to changing the story. They created a narrative in which what they did to you was not their fault.

Most of the time, it was probably easiest to make it your fault. After all, you were emotionally attached to them, so you were an easy target for this narrative.

It was your fault they failed socially or did not know how to act accordingly. They had to convince themselves and you that it was your fault because they never learned how to handle anything being their own fault.

Boundary Violation: The Narcissist Neither Understands nor Respects Them

One thing narcissists typically struggle with is the keeping of boundaries. It is likely that their boundaries were violated by the narcissist that raised them. For this or whatever reason, the narcissist you were to never developed a sense of boundaries. This might not have been a cause for the issue if the person could have understood your boundaries or learned to respect them at least.

Unfortunately, the boundaries are a difficult concept for a narcissist to grasp. In truth, this can be a seductive and alluring aspect of a narcissist. You might have felt instantly connected to this narcissist because you felt the absence of boundaries. Perhaps, at first, this felt like a very good and intimate thing. Perhaps it was. Yet, it is likely that he became confusing for you eventually.

At some point, your ability to remove your own boundaries was probably tested. The truth is shame and boundaries serve a purpose in human relationships. The narcissist probably made you feel ashamed of your boundaries when, in reality, you both should have respected your boundaries. It might take a little work for you to reclaim your boundaries accordingly.

Reciprocation: The Narcissist Does Not Reciprocate

The other, perhaps obvious, form of abuse you experienced in your relationship with a narcissist was a lack of reciprocation. You need to go back and consider how true this is on your relationship. Perhaps the narcissist you were with tried, but failed, or perhaps never really tried. In the end, the point is that your relationship lacked reciprocation, or else you would probably not be reading this book. The lack of reciprocation you experienced means your recovery is going to require a reevaluation of what reciprocation means to you.

The reason, in case you're interested that the narcissist you were with was unable to reciprocate appropriately, is because of their sense of entitlement. Their sense of entitlement made it so that they believed they deserved everything you gave them without the requirement of reciprocation. In fact, they probably believed they deserved more than you could give them.

Narcissists have a sense of entitlement to riches, fame, and glamour that is completely unearned and unjustified. You might give them everything you can make them "feel like a princess," but if you are not buying tiaras, you are probably not doing anything like what an entitled narcissist believes they deserve. This is not your fault, but it is an explanation as to why you received such insufficient reciprocation.

Chapter 3: Acknowledging Abuse and Setting Your Intention Toward Recovery

You may have heard that you can't find love until you learn to love yourself. This is often true of most things. You can't learn to be patient with others until you learn to be patient with yourself. Sure, you might be more patient with others than you are yourself already. Yet, you'll find that when you fail at being patient with others, it is most likely a failure because you have absolutely no patience with yourself when it comes to that particular kind of mistake.

I have a family member who is *always* early to everything. That same family member has absolutely no patience for tardiness. I am sure you have examples like this as well. The point is that we often have less patience for others when it comes to matters of which we are not patient with ourselves. One way to find patience with yourself is to ask yourself about your own intentions.

Often times, we request forgiveness because our intention was not aimed toward harm. You might say you're sorry, but you did not mean to offend. What you mean is that it was not your intention to offend. In this case, you apologize and request forgiveness for that apology based upon the explanation that you did not mean to offend.

When you make a mistake, ask yourself if you meant to make that mistake. If you did, you might have some further reckoning to do with yourself. If you didn't, you might approach yourself the way you would approach someone else who made an unintentional mistake. Or, you could approach yourself the way you would want someone else to approach your unintentional mistake—with forgiveness.

It's a strange thought, I realize. Being patient with others requires learning to be patient with yourself, and being patient with yourself requires treating yourself with the kind of patience you treat others. It seems paradoxical, I know. What it actually accomplishes, however, is the resolution of a paradox.

A paradox is something that seems contradictory, but somehow is not. It seems contradictory that you'd need to learn to be patient with yourself to be patient with others because you're naturally more patient with others. It isn't actually a contradiction, though.

It means that if you take your more natural disposition to be patient and apply it to yourself, you'll be even *more* patient with others because you'll resolve those instances of complete inability to be patient with yourself. You'll resolve your failures in times of patience.

Again, your failures when it comes to patience can usually be linked to those instances in which you afford yourself no patience. If you can afford yourself no patience for delay, you will be unable to provide others' patience either. This isn't necessarily a bad thing. You could live a completely fulfilled life without patience for tardiness. The point is not about the matter.

The point is that the more patience you show yourself, the more patience you'll show others. Since you naturally show more patience to others than yourself, show yourself the kind of patience you show others. Once you've allowed yourself more patience, you will find you have more patience for others. It's that simple (or, that complicated). In either case, you can do it.

There is a multitude of activities you can do to improve upon your patience with yourself. This is crucial to your ability to recover and develop new relationships.

You must learn to guard yourself against entering into another relationship with a narcissist, but it is also important that you do not become so impatient with anything that reminds you of the narcissist in your last relationship that you struggle to form new relationships.

The world is a more stimulating place than the narcissist you were with made it feel. You will need to come up with new activities to find yourself in the world again. The relationship you were in with a narcissist attacked your sense of identity, boundaries, reality, and control. You will need to actively participate in activities that put you back to a place where you can reclaim your sense of identity and control.

Your goal is to find activities to reestablish what was taken from you. You will want to reestablish your boundaries. You will want to reclaim your identity. You will want to find a relationship in which reciprocation is readily available and understood as important.

You have the tools in your home, neighborhood, and backyard to reestablish your boundaries. Actively pursue the reinstatement of your boundaries. You have the tools to reclaim your identity. Actively pursue your own sense of self. Recognize how it was stifled and how you can get it back.

Admitting that there has been a problem in your life that caused you to lose your sense of identity will be crucial for your recovery. You must get out into the world and find your place again. You must reclaim it without the narcissist you were in a relationship with previously.

Yoga is a great way to stimulate a fruitful connection between mind, body, and one's surroundings in people who might not be ready to become active in traditional sports and other such strenuous activities. This is the perfect example of a theme you could take so far beyond the ten poses offered in this book.

The ten poses offered were selected because they promote mindfulness, which will help you reclaim your identity as you work toward a mindfulness of yourself and your body's needs. The narcissist you were in a relationship with disrespected your body's boundaries and your mind's need for human connection and grounding in reality. It is time for you to find activities that tie you to the ground again and help you look inward.

Like yoga or anything else, mindfulness can be practiced and honed; it just takes a conscious effort. Conscientiousness is mindfulness, after all. You will hone mindfulness as soon as you start doing activities for yourself again. You simply have to do the work to articulate the experience and provide yourself with the understanding that you are doing things for yourself again.

These activities are meant to give you ideas to instigate theses experience and to inspire reclamation of identity. Use them well, but feel free to create your own experiences along the way. The point is simply to get started conscientiously.
You'll find that mindfulness/conscientiousness inspires self-reflection. If you have wondered how anyone can teach self-reflection, you've asked a great question. Some people seem to be turned inward. Others seem to be turned outward. We all seem to have the potential to change our gaze, though.

When you were with a narcissist both of you gazed into them. Now it is time for you to start practicing gazing inward toward yourself and then outward toward other things than the narcissist that convinced you that your gaze was most worthwhile when it was on them.

Self-awareness is an important part of life. Children become self-conscious at a scary point in their life. We use the word self-conscious colloquially to mean something like bashful or socially anxious. Its literal meaning is essential to be self-aware—to be aware of one's self as a self. Any child will become self-aware and self-conscious (both meanings now apply) without much warning. It is important that, when this happens, they know how to self-reflect and then speak to others about their self-reflections.

This is how we move between turning inward and turning outward. What you will be learning to do once again is honor your self-awareness and your ability to turn inward and outward. The reason for this is that you have had your gaze turned toward the narcissist for a long time. It is time to turn it toward yourself and others.

Some people get stuck in their inward lives. Struggles that result from this are numerous. This can make relationships challenging. It can make holding a job challenging. It is crucial to your recovery that you neither get stuck retreating back into yourself nor outward without reclaiming your sense of identity. The narcissist you were with was empty inside. He or she tried to empty you out too. Don't be like them. You have to find the substance within yourself without forgetting to do what the narcissist struggled to do—look outside of yourself too. You need to make these passages. You need to find yourself without getting stuck there.

The walks in nature will pull you outward. The daily tasks listed in the following chapters will make you self-aware and test your ability to turn your sights toward something in the world. It will make you remember how to be more aware of your own body and your boundaries.

The point involved in all of the activities listed in the coming chapters is to help you turn into yourself and out of yourself while reclaiming your identity and regaining your control. You need to recover actively. Your abuse was experienced passively. It is time to be active now.

Technology is precisely mediation, which makes it the opposite of immediacy. Technology is a go-between. Someone creates something for us. We do not have to engage in the world directly. We get to do it directly. We may not be able to speak with someone directly, but with a social media app, we can speak with them indirectly.

We can even spy on someone, making the experience overtly indirect. They don't have to know we are looking into their lives and interests because we can peek into their lives and interests indirectly.

Overall, this book encourages more direct interaction between you and your world. One point these activities will continue to stress is that you actively consider yourself to be working toward your recovery every day that you are no longer in a relationship with a narcissist. So, of course, the first step is making sure this book is right for you. Hopefully, the first couple of chapters have helped you establish whether or not you were, in fact, in a relationship with a narcissist.

The last chapter acknowledged why you might not have been certain about whether or not the narcissist you were in a relationship perfectly fit the textbook examples of a narcissist. You might have thought you were in a relationship with a narcissist, but felt that the narcissist you were with knew how to hide being a narcissist at times.

The truth is that narcissists are good at hiding what they are ashamed of. They cannot handle shame, so they do not want to feel it. They will avoid it. If they were ashamed of their parent who was a narcissist, they might be especially good at hiding. You must think of the surprise outbursts and the abuse you did experience. Otherwise, you won't ever feel like you're reading the right book.

If you are sure by now that you were in a relationship with a narcissist, regardless of their ability to hide it from you occasionally, it is time for you to move towards acceptance of your abuse. Only once you accept the abuse, you experienced can you move past it. It is time for you to acknowledge it and face reality in the way the narcissist could not.

You must undo the issues they caused due to the issues they had. First, you should realize that they may have passed on some of their tendencies to you. In other words, you might also now experience a difficulty to deal with shame, accept reality, put up boundaries, and have reciprocal relationships. You will need to get over these issues in order to recover.

Your Reaction to Shame After Narcissistic Abuse

Depending upon how long you were with a narcissist, you may have picked up on their defense mechanisms when it comes to shame. You might now be experiencing a kind of a shame you are no better equipped to deal with than the narcissist was. You might be ashamed of yourself to falling victim to a narcissist. This is understandable.

If you have been reading this book and thinking on the one hand that you were definitely in a relationship with a narcissist and that, on the other hand, it was never as obvious then as it is now, it is important that you learn to accept that you are not special.

Your relationship with a narcissist was no more special than the narcissist was. A narcissist thinks they're special. If you think your relationship with this particular narcissist was special, you have fallen victim to thinking like the narcissist you were with wanted you to think.

Acknowledge the reality of your relationship. It was great at first. Narcissists are attractive for many reasons. Forgive yourself for being attracted. It's an attractive thing. Narcissists appear seductively aloof. Their lack of boundaries appears intimate.

Their unquenchable thirst for affirmation makes them appear as though they simply need your love to be whole. If you're an empath, you had every reason to want to help the narcissist you were in a relationship. It is important that you realize that you were duped, but that doesn't mean you have to hate yourself.

Admit it. You aren't special. Your relationship with a narcissist was not special. No one is that special. If you were really special, you would hear all of this from someone more important than the author of this book. The point of accepting this is avoiding the sins of narcissism yourself.

The narcissist you were with could have been really good at tricking you, but that does not mean that you were not tricked. Admit that you are "trickable." Admit that you are fallible. Admit that you are human. Accept this and get ready to move on. Don't be a narcissist. Don't deny your reality.

If this abuse fits your experience, accept that and learn to move on. If you keep criticizing books because they don't describe a narcissist as talented as yours, you aren't helping yourself. You're falling victim to narcissistic thinking. Accept the reality of your situation so that you can move on in a way that they can't.

Your New Tendency to Distort Reality

If you aren't able to accept that you were abused, and instead come up with a new reality in which your relationship was special, you won't move on. Maybe your relationship was fine. Don't read this book in this case. If you really want to recover, however, you need to accept that your relationship with a narcissist was not special—it was what it was. Whatever it was, whatever abuse you suffered, accept it. Recover from it as needed.

Don't distort the reality of what you went through. You have to accept it. You can't spend the entire time you're devoting to reading this book, rejecting it because the narcissist you were with was slightly different. Either you were with a narcissist, or you were not.

If you were not, you have read too far already. If you were, keep reading and keep healing. You deserve it. You are not entitled to the way the narcissist you were with believing themselves to be, but you do deserve a sense of self, a sense of boundaries, and a sense of control. Accept what you've been through. Leave your pride at bay. Move one.

Feel shame. Go ahead. Feel ashamed that you were in a relationship with a narcissist. Feel bad that you were tricked. Feel bad that you were duped. It is not that big of a deal. Feel shame because you can. Feel shame because you are not a narcissist. Feel shame because shame is good. Feel shame, accept blame, and move on.

The longer you deny your responsibility, the longer you will take to recover. Accept your part in the matter. It isn't that big of a deal. You're still amazing because you, unlike your partner, are taking steps toward recovery.

Your New Difficulty With Boundaries
You might be establishing your boundaries like a tyrant now. Be careful. It's understandable that you feel the need to never let anyone cross your boundaries ever again, but try not to over-correct. Part of your recovery will involve a reciprocal relationship with established

boundaries. It is important that you communicate boundaries.

It is also important that you don't let yourself become a tyrant. Understand that though narcissists will tend to violate boundaries, boundary violators are not necessarily narcissists.

You want to have a healthy relationship now. That doesn't mean you enforce boundaries with the rigor the narcissist you were with violated them. This means that you learn how to communicate about boundaries with someone who also understands and respects them.

Understanding and respecting boundaries do not mean you, and another person instantly knows each other's boundaries. It means you learn them and that, once you learn them, you do your best to respect them. This is all that can be reasonably expected in a relationship. Even so, this will be a step up from where you were with a narcissist.

Your New Difficulty to Reciprocate

Reciprocation is important. You need to establish your own understanding of what reciprocation means, what you were lacking, and what you want in the future. Just like what was said in the previous section about boundaries, communication is the key.

You don't get to be in a relationship with a non-narcissist who immediately understands reciprocation the same way you do. But you do get to discuss reciprocation with the next person you are with and make sure you two have a similar understanding of what reciprocation means and how important it is in a relationship.

Do not get used to the idea of a lack of reciprocation. It is important that you establish reciprocation in relationships in order for you to recover. Without the experience of reciprocation, you will not change your course of relationships.

If you get back into a relationship wherein you are doing all of the work and your partner is not expected to do any of it, you might as well be back in a relationship with a narcissist. You must communicate your needs to the person you're with. Communicate why you do what you do for the other person. Communicate what you would like done for you.

Again, you cannot expect that the person you are with is going to be everything you need. What you can expect is that the right person will hear you when you ask for what you need. You will know you are in a healthier relationship when expressing your needs leads to a conversation instead of an argument.

If you were in a relationship with a narcissist, expressing your needs was always met with resistance. In a better relationship, expressing your needs will be met with a conversation. There will be a noticeable difference. You and they deserve that conversation. Everyone deserves a conversation after they express their needs.

Needs are not easy to express. If you can learn to express your needs to the next person you are with, you are on the right track to recovery. If you are with the right person to move toward your recovery, they will commend your expression of needs and be willing to have a conversation about them even if a disagreement is involved.

If you were with a narcissist, you became accustomed to outbursts when you expressed that your needs were not being met. If you are in a healthy relationship, your partner will want your needs to be met concerning their own needs. This is what reciprocation is.

Your partner should not be willing to sacrifice themselves and their needs to meet yours. If that is happening, you have over-corrected and found someone with an equally difficult complication as the narcissist you were with. The right person for your recovery will have their own boundaries and their own needs, which they will readily express to you.

You must be better than a narcissist when they do express these needs to you. You cannot ignore them as if the fact that they have needs makes them a narcissist. You must embrace the fact that both of you have needs.

It is okay that you both have needs. In fact, it is the only way a real relationship works. You both need to be okay with the fact that each of you has needs. You both need to be okay with the fact that both of you have boundaries. If you are, you should be able to communicate. You should be able to establish respect. You should be able to recover from your past relationships.

You should be able to be good for each other. You should be able to help each other as well as yourselves. You should be able to feel better with each other than without. You should feel like yourself again with this person.

So, proceed to the next chapters to find recommendations for activities that will promote your recovery, reclamation of identity, and regaining of control. Tailor these activities to be your own. Keep in mind that the point is always to make you feel more like yourself again.

The point is to establish your boundaries. The point is to turn outward and inward. The point is to feel in control of yourself and your surroundings to an appropriate extent. The narcissist might benefit from these activities too, but we are no longer worried about them. We are only concerned with you and your recovery.

Chapter 4: Recommended Activities for Recovery

This chapter offers some ideas that will help you get out into the world while you work toward recovery. Though you can do a lot to prompt your recovery by reading, as you are doing, at some point, you need to leave your comfort zone and establish your recovery by being active with your body.

This chapter will talk about the benefits of going on walks and doing yoga. If you are already the athletic type, you may need to find greater challenges. If you already go for daily walks and/or runs and do yoga, your recovery might require a more drastic alteration in your activity level.

The point is that it is important to be active in order to recover. If you don't put your body in motion, it will never be in motion. If it never is in motion, it will never stay in motion. Don't get stuck. Your relationship with a narcissist was all about making you feel stuck. You felt tied to them. You felt tied to their approval.

You felt tied to doing things their way. Now, you need to actively pursue your own activities. Right now, depending on your stage of recovery, going for a walk every day and doing a few yoga poses before bed might make a world of difference.

If you already think that you will need more than a walk or some yoga to prompt your recovery, you may want to join some sort of trendy fitness group that will really get you going and challenge you in healthy ways.

Maybe you need to start doing Crossfit or Pilates. Maybe you need to teach fitness classes again. Maybe you need to go back to doing whatever kind of fitness the narcissist in your life put down. If the narcissist you were in a relationship thought yoga was garbage, yoga might be exactly what you need to do to prompt your recovery and regain control.

The point of this introduction to the chapter is to acknowledge that walks and yoga might not be the perfect solutions for everyone, but the ideas being presented in the benefits of these activities will carry over in whatever it is you decide to do to feel present in your own body again.

Keep in mind that walks and yoga are good supplements, however. The following activities might not be sufficient for you, but that doesn't mean they aren't beneficial. Part of the reason for these activities is to make you feel like you're actively part of the world again (not just the world of the narcissist you were with).

Part of the reason for these activities is to help you learn how to relax again. Think about how often the narcissist you were with wanted you to relax. Think about how much the narcissist you were to affect your approach to relaxation.

It might be necessary for you to reevaluate how you feel about relaxation. One thing worth keeping in mind as you approach these activities is that their purpose is to help you relax because relaxation is a key component for recovery.

Going on Walks

Going on walks is excellent for recovery; age does not matter. If some aid is necessary, use one. Whether you're single and need to spend some time walking alone or with a partner, a walk is a good way to process the day. Partners should go on walks to talk about their lives and to observe the seasons together.

Walks inspire questions about nature, which makes us turn our gaze outward. We get to step away from ourselves, which gives us the kind of distance that is necessary for recovery. Walks are an opportunity for you to teach yourself nature. If you come up with questions you do not have the answer to, you should make it a project for yourself to discover the answer.

One activity while walking is to observe the trees and the effects of the seasonal changes. If you walk frequently enough, you will be able to bear witness to the changes of the seasons. Observe the changes in the leaves if there are leaves.

If it is winter, consider what the absence of leaves means for the animals and insects that spend time in trees. Get outside of yourself on these walks. Getting out of yourself and into nature will give you a new perspective on yourself the next time you take a look inward.

The second activity is journaling. You could bring along a notepad or journal and write down questions you have about plants, animals, and trees you see. The other day my mother and I struggled to recall the name for Spanish Broom.
It took up much of the conversation along our walk. We were pleased when she finally recalled the name for the lovely bushes filled with fragrant yellow flowers that appear to have bloomed late this year.

A third activity is stopping to smell the roses. Actually, it is stopping to take a closer look at anything that inspires interest at all. Make the mission of a walk the walk itself, not the conclusion of a walk. Find enjoyment in the journey. Take breaks. Stop and see. Stop and smell. Stop and touch. Stop and talk.

The fourth activity that follows from the previous one is to make a note of the stops you make and ask yourself why you've stopped. It is important to get away from yourself by looking at nature but also important to remember to look inward from time to time.

You might learn interesting things about yourself by noticing what makes you stop in order to get a closer look. The ultimate goal of the previous activity and this one is to encourage your stopping to look.

The difference is that this activity also encourages you to ask why you stopped to investigate a particular thing. This is a cause for self-reflection. Why does the Spanish Broom interest you more than the mailbox next to it? Or is it the cat in the window that has your attention?

The fifth activity is observing the weather. An obvious start is assessing the current weather activity. A more in-depth analysis is asking what purposes changes in weather might mean on a cosmic level.

The narcissist you were in a relationship made you feel small so that they could feel big. When you think about the cosmos, no human being stands as tall as the narcissist made you think they did. Thinking about the cosmos debunks the myth, they tried to make you believe about their greatness.

The sixth activity is skipping. It has come to my intention that fewer and fewer people know the joys of skipping. It is essential to check in on one's coordination. Skipping is often as fun as it is fundamentally useful in developing one's motor skills. Skip to acknowledging the rhythm of your body as it moves following the ground below it, resisting and accepting the pull of gravity.

The seventh activity is jumping over the cracks in the sidewalk. Part of developing mindfulness and self-awareness is doing an activity out of awareness of one's surroundings and interact with one's surroundings. Jumping over cracks in the sidewalk makes one aware of the ground one walks on.

It's perfectly understandable if civilization has made you too embarrassed to do skip or jump over the cracks. Find a private place for these activities in that case. Or, if you have a child, do these activities with them. It will be good for both of you.

The eighth activity is listening. Walking and talking are great, but silence during a walk is advantageous, too. Challenge yourself to listen to your surroundings. Then, if you're on an accompanied walk, invite talking once more and discuss what you heard.

The ninth activity is closing your eyes and trying to remember what your surroundings are. Walk to a certain spot and stop. Cover your eyes and recall what you've just seen in front of you. If you begin to get good at this activity, start asking yourself to remember what is to the left of you, right of you, and behind you.

The tenth activity follows the walk. Put your arms above your head and breathe deeply. Try to relax more with every breath. Learning how to relax is one of the most important parts of your recovery. Narcissists are often exciting and energizing because they need so much of you.

It can become addicting to feel that you must never relax because of this. So, in order to recover, you must learn to relax. For this reason, the next section is on yoga. Yoga, when properly practiced, is a helpful way to relax, meditate, and recover from just about anything.

Playing With Yoga Poses

Yoga poses are cleverly and playfully named to attach themselves poses found in nature. Some of them refer to human poses, such as Dancer and Happy Baby. Others refer to animals, such as Downward Dog and Pigeon.

Doing these poses creates body-awareness. Here are ten yoga poses that have been said to promote healing.

One pose is Child's Pose (Balsana). Allowing your lungs to expand improves the flow of oxygen to your brain. The child's pose is for resting. It is best to rest and breath in this pose. In the child's pose, your shin, palms, and forehead rest on the ground. Your spine curves. Your chest rests on the top of your thighs. If you have any knee or hip issues, spread your knees farther apart.

The second pose is Hero's Pose (Virasana). Leaving your legs as they are in Child's pose, lengthen your upper body and rise until the crown of your head is directly above your hips, and your spine is straight.

Breathe deeply and allow the shoulders to fall. Keep reaching the crown of the head to the sky. Consider the names of the poses. Consider if you feel safe or vulnerable in Child's Pose. Consider if you feel powerful in Hero's Pose. Be mindful of your body. Be mindful of yourself.

The third pose is Mountain Pose (Tadasana). Mountain Pose is a powerful pose. Rise from the ground, from Child's Pose and Hero's pose, and stand tall. Continue reaching the crown of the head to the sky but with the full extension of your legs supporting you now. Open the palms to receive energy.

Close your eyes. As we age, sitting in Child's Pose and Hero's Pose can be strenuous if our muscles are tight in certain places. You should not have this issue in Mountain Pose. The struggle you might run into in Mountain Pose is losing your balance once your eyes are closed. Acknowledge the connection between the functioning of your body and your sense perception. Find your balance. Maintain it as long as you can.

The fourth pose is Tree Pose (Vriksasana). From Mountain Pose, you can practice balancing on one leg. First, play with the foot that will remain on the ground. See how well you can spread your toes. The wider you spread your toes, the more rooted you will be in the ground. Once you have rooted yourself with the foot you will stand on, begin to lift the other foot. It is totally fine if you are unable to place your foot on the inside of your thigh. Start by trying to place the toes of your lifted foot on the ankle of your grounded foot. If you find this to be quite easy, keep inching the lifted foot higher. The goal is to get the toes of the lifted foot above the knee of the rooted leg. The inside of your lifted leg should face forward, creating a figure-four with your legs. Once you are satisfied with your attempts on one leg, do the other!

The fifth pose is Bow Pose (Dhanurasana). Shake out those legs and ankles after playing with your balance and return to the ground, this time, lie flat on your stomachs. Try to bring your ankles as close as you can to your backside. Again, play with the name. Consider how this pose is similar to the bow of a bow-and-arrow. Reach to grab your toes, feet or ankles. Then, create the kind of resistance one creates when one stretches a bow in order to release an arrow. Acknowledge the tension you have created in this pose. Allow yourself to play in this pose. If you can, roll a little on your stomach. Play is important for recovery.

The sixth pose is Cobra Pose (Bhujangasana). Of course, this is another great name worth thinking about. Consider how this pose resembles a cobra. Since you're already on your stomach, having released yourselves from Bow Pose, place your palms flat on the ground beside your ribcage and push with the full extension of your triceps. Remember always, to breathe. Play with your breathing, in fact. If it feels good, breathe as loudly as you can. You may enjoy it more than you'd expect.

The seventh pose is Camel Pose (Ustrasana). Slowly bring yourself out of Cobra Pose. Feel out Child's Pose and Hero's Pose once more. From Hero's Pose, reach back for your ankles and let your heart shine toward the sky. Allow your spine to curve in the opposite direction from Child's Pose but mainly from the upper part of your back, expanding your ribcage. Breathe. Imagine becoming the hump of a camel. See how easy it is to escape in the mind when the body is part of the imagining.

The eighth pose is Table Top Pose (Bharmanasana). Keep your shins on the ground as they have been in

Child's Pose, Hero's Pose, and Camel Pose. Place your palms flat on the ground directly below your shoulders. Play with this. Imagine someone is placing a coaster (or some other extremely light object) on your back to see if your back is indeed like a tabletop.

The ninth pose is Cow Pose (Bitilasana). From Table Top Pose, inhale deeply and drop your belly to the mat as the crown of your head begins to lift upward. You should feel as though your belly is sinking to the ground like the udders of a dairy cow. This thought may cause some laughing, which will only improve upon the effects of the pose and the benefits of this practice. Laughter is also a source of healing.

The tenth pose, the Cat Pose (Marjaryasana). From Cow Pose, exhale deeply and begin to drop your head as your spine curves in the opposite direction, and your belly button lifts higher and higher. Let your head hang heavily. Go ahead and hiss like a mad cat as you exhale. Again, play is essential. Enjoy yourself. Play with language. Play with poses. Make a play of your yoga practice. The narcissist you were in a relationship may or may not have been inviting of your playfulness. You must regain this if you've lost it. If they were inviting of only certain kinds of playfulness, consider the kinds you would like to now include on your own terms.

If you find either or both of these activities are helping, but you would like to take them further, turn them into social activities. Invite more people on your walks. Go for walks more often. Find a place to really hike. Travel a little for a good hike. Find a yoga class. Invite someone you enjoy spending time with to try a yoga class with you. If you aren't quite ready to leave the comfort of your own home for yoga, buy a DVD, and invite a friend over to do yoga with you. It will be good for your recovery if you start inviting other people to join in. You will become stronger as you identify your activity with your recovery and share your experience with others.

Yet, remember that the point is not to tell others they need to do this activity with you so that they can also recover. The point is to share in the activity that is helping you recover without having to explain the process to anyone else unless they are particularly interested.

In sharing this activity, you will identify it as yours. Such accomplishments will jumpstart your next task, which is to reclaim your identity. It is one thing to beginning healing on solitary walks and your yoga practice. It is another to begin re-entering your social world in light of your path toward recovery.

You must re-enter your social world in this new light so that you may reclaim your identity within the social world. Bringing the social world into the safety of your recovery zone will be a bridge to that next step. Use this bridge to become comfortable and familiar with working toward your recovery in front of others.

You cannot hide from the world while you recover. Your recovery must take place in the world so that you can reclaim your place within it. You don't want to abandon the good things you had going for you even while you were in a relationship with a narcissist. Keep what is good in your life around. If you are not sure at first what that is, your meditation on walks and during yoga should help you figure it out.

The next chapter offers more activities with an eye toward reclaiming your identity. The narcissist you were in a relationship probably did their best to deny you your identity. Once you're on your path to recovery, reclaiming your identity might feel like a difficult detour.

The reason of this is that the narcissist you were with, probably did a substantial amount of damage to your sense of self. The activities in the next chapter will help you engage your senses until your sense of self has been rejuvenated.

Chapter 5: Recommended Activities for Reclaiming Your Identity

If you have been in a relationship with a narcissist, you have lost some sense of your own identity because that narcissist tried to make you part of their identity. Narcissists have issues with boundaries, so they saw you as an extension of themselves. Being treated as if you were an extension of someone else is bound to have made you feel less like yourself. You should not have to feel that way anymore. You should be able to feel like yourself again.

The activities in this chapter are geared toward helping you do this productively and without having to do anything too extreme. The main components of these activities have to do with asking yourself meaningful questions, coming up with meaningful answers, and exploring your sense perceptions until you revitalize your sense of self.

As is true of all of these chapters, these activities may not be sufficient. You might still need therapy to really get a sense of who you are after your relationship with a narcissist. Even so, these activities will not harm you. They will help you recover.

Interviewing Yourself

Sometimes it is hard to ask the right questions. Sometimes an open-ended question like "How was your day?" is too quickly answered with a single word like, "Fine." The art of the interview is to ask the kinds of questions that require fleshed out responses that bring about new questions. Interview yourself and get them comfortable asking yourself what you think about the matter at hand. An interview requires self-reflection and a sense of identity.

One activity involved in the interviewing process is coming up with the right questions to ask. Think about what kinds of questions you wish someone would ask you. Think about the kinds of questions you ask other people naturally.

Guide yourself through the process of formulating questions as if you were guiding someone else preparing an interview for you. Acknowledge the difference between open-ended questions and closed questions. Then, make a list of open-ended questions to which only you have the answers.

A second activity that follows right along from the previous one is coming up with a list of questions to ask someone else. To make this a team effort, ask someone else what kinds of questions they would like for you to ask them. Or, ask them what kinds of questions they would like to be asked if they were interviewed.

Think about the differences between the kinds of questions they wish to be asked and the kinds of questions you would like to be asked. Think about how these things make you different kinds of people and have to do with your different identities and personalities.

A third activity is asking other people the kinds of questions you asked yourself. Just like in the last activity, you can acknowledge the differences between their answers and your answers.

For a fourth activity, you might even go ahead and guess the answers you would expect to hear from them before you ask. See if they surprise you. Consider how much of your thoughts, desires, and personality traits went into your guesswork.

Consider how faulty your guesswork might be if you aren't answering questions because you assume you know the answers. Acknowledge the differences between your guesses and the answers.

A fifth activity is to discuss your guesswork with the other person. Discuss the benefits of anticipating answers. Discuss the possible negative effects of anticipating answers. Discuss when it is best to ask, even if one thinks one knows the answer.

A sixth activity is writing or typing out your answer to a question you found particularly interesting. This could be the answer someone else gave you to a question that you thought was strange because it was so different from yours. This could be an answer you came up with that surprised even you. The point is just to sit down and give a little more thought to this activity by writing or typing it out.

A seventh activity is actually recording yourself as if you were responding to an interview question and then watching that recording. See how you express yourself. See if the person in the recording looks different than the person you generally believe yourself to be.

If you think it might be helpful, ask yourself how the narcissist you were with saw you. Consider the difference between all of these different notions of yourself. Finally, think about who you want to be.

An eighth activity is finding someone else to interview over Snapchat or some social media app like that. It is pretty easy to send someone a video asking them an open-ended question. Play around with this and observe how the two of you express yourself when being questioned and having a little time to watch yourself send each other recorded responses. Get to know yourself the way someone who communicates with you through such means would know you.

A ninth activity is revisiting the previous discussion about anticipating answers. Once you have spent a little more time playing around with these interview-style conversations, think about how much you learned that you could never have guessed. Apply this to yourself now. Do you ever make assumptions about yourself that turn out not to be true? Surely you have guessed that you would not like something that you turned out to like more than expected.

A tenth activity is to reflect on the difference between casual conversation and an interview. Consider what you have learned about your identity. Consider how to keep this practice going in a way that is healthy and helpful to you. It does not have to be as formal as the descriptions above.

The point is to start asking yourself and other meaningful questions that you can learn from, but you must be active about getting started. The casual conversation has a way of being the default, most of the time.

The next section is more about exploring your sense perceptions. Step out of your mind and get back into your body. Learn to attach your body and mind to your sense of identity. The activities provided are meant to get you feeling more connected to the world through your own unique sense perceptions. The endgame, of course, is to gain a better sense of self. Once you've gained a better sense of self, you may reclaim your identity as you wish.

Reinvigorating Your Sense Perceptions

Considering the power of one's own power of senses promotes self-awareness.

One well-known activity that concerns the sense of sight is the game I-Spy. You should play I-Spy with yourself to awaken your interactive sense of sight. Select one thing that you see and study that thing with your eyes. See how your eyes focus. See how difficult it is for you to focus on one thing. See how long you can focus on that one thing. See if you learn anything from focusing on that one thing.

A second activity is to make an I-Hear version of I-Spy. Follow the same instructions. Be quiet. Try to tune into one thing. Listen to it as well as you can. Listen to it as long as you can. Listen to something else if something else becomes too loud to hear the last thing you tried to listen to. Just try to close your eyes and listen to something, anything.

A third activity is to make an I-Touch version of I-Spy. Touch something that feels good. Think about why it feels good. Think about the appropriate ways to touch that thing that feels good. Think about gentleness and what it means. Think about your ability to be gentle. Feel good about yourself for being able to touch something gently.

A fourth activity is to turn I-Spy into I-Smell. This one will be particularly fun in the kitchen or the backyard. The same rules apply. Choose one smell. Think about how you would explain a single smell to someone who had never smelled that thing before. You might notice that smells are nearly impossible to describe without simply comparing to other smells.

A fifth activity is to turn I-Spy into I-Taste. This might be fun to do with some kind of baked goods or anything with complicated ingredients. Try to guess what each ingredient is. See how advanced your palate is.

A sixth activity is to play I-Spy with you in the mirror. Look at yourself. What do you see? Find one thing to focus on. Focus on it until it means something new to you than it did before. Give some aspect of you the kind of attention you spent on the narcissist you were with. Determine that this part of you deserves this kind of attention.

A seventh activity is to play I-Hear with your own voice. Say something that you would like to hear yourself say. Focus on the way it sounds when you say it. If you don't like the way it sounds at first, say it until you do like the way it sounds. Once you've figured out how to say it the way you want it to sound, repeat it like that several times.

An eighth activity is to play I-Smell with your own hair, room, or otherwise personal kind of aroma. Find a smell that you find particularly pleasant that has to do with you. It should be a smell that you identify with, or someone has identified with you. Smell it as such. Think about how this smell is related to you, your space, and your identity.

A ninth activity is to play I-touch with your own body or personal space. Find something to touch that is either on your person or in your personal space. Touch it gently. Think about how it feels. Once again, be sure that you are giving the kind of attention you used to give to the narcissist to whatever it is you are touching. Remember how whatever you are touching is tied to your identity. Think about what this means to you.

A tenth activity is to play I-taste with your own cooking and knowing the ingredients you used. Cook something you love to eat. Think about every ingredient. When you taste it, try to recall each ingredient. See if you can taste each ingredient. Give yourself credit for your work. Appreciate the work you've done in the way you always hoped to receive appreciation from the narcissist you were within a relationship.

Therapy

You must go to therapy for help reclaiming your identity. Therapy is one place that is guaranteed to be all about your project of learning how to be yourself and live productively with yourself and others.

Identifying your personal struggles will be welcomed and safely guided by someone familiar with narcissistic abuse. Your therapist will give you options that are tailored to your personal needs based on the type of abuse you experienced.

Counseling sessions are good for providing relief and emotional catharsis as well as proper guidance toward healing and recovery. If your goal is to reclaim your identity, you should tell your therapist about your intention. Therapy will be a place where you can safely share your experience of narcissistic abuse while making your way toward recovery. You will receive affirmation that what you experienced was, in fact, damage from a person with a narcissistic personality disorder. Your therapist may even be open to helping you better understand the narcissist you were in a relationship if you and your therapist decide it would be helpful for you.

Therapy is all about reclaiming one's identity because everything about it is geared toward the betterment of the patient. Therapy is one place where you know it will be all about you, which is a big step from where you were when you were with a narcissist.

When you were with a narcissist, it was all about them. The best way for you to start recovering and reclaiming your identity is to find a place where it can be all about you for an hour or so. You may not be comfortable making it all about you at first, but you will find that it is helpful to do so. You may have lost a lot of yourself. Finding yourself may require a little help from a professional.

That said, the activities in this book should continue to help you with or without therapy. You will be better off with these activities than without making any moves toward your recovery.

You will be better off using these activities to supplement the work you are doing in therapy. Make sure you find the right therapist. Therapists are usually more than willing to help you find the right person even if it turns out they are not the right person for you.

Don't be afraid to tell the first therapist you try that you might be looking for something else. They'll be glad to help you find what you're looking for. Remember that there are a lot of different kinds of therapy and counseling for you to seek and settle into.

Chapter 6: Recommended Activities for Regaining Control

Interacting With Pets

A beloved professor of mine said parents needed to make sure their children get the experience of having pets. Pets teach us about nature, life, death, and responsibility. Pets inspire questions. They make us want to understand why a hamster would eat its children, why a snake tortures its food, or why a housecat still hunts even though it isn't hungry. There are lessons in nature. Having pets puts those lessons in the living room, or at least, in the backyard.

One activity worth considering as you try to regain control over your own thoughts is imagining what one's pets are thinking. The neatest thing about this activity is that it urges us to think about thinking. From this activity, you could consider questions as in-depth as asking what the nature of thought is and whether or not non-human animals do an activity like the one we call thinking. Or, your thoughts can stay as light as considering why one's kitten is looking in a certain direction or what it thinks is beneath the blanket when we put our hand under it.

A second activity is imagining how your pets would speak if they could speak English. This activity follows nicely from the previous one. Now that you have considered the desires and instincts related to the human notion of thinking, you can wonder how your kitten (or any other pet) would express itself if it could speak in English. Would it speak in complete sentences or partial ones? Which thoughts, would it choose to convey to its owners?

A third activity is trying to communicate with one's pets. Again, this activity follows well from the previous activities. Once you have considered what a pet might think or feel and how a pet might communicate, you should see how you might communicate with your pet. This will allow you to explore the nature of communication and how much communication is in the linguistic environment.

Of course, linguistic communication is off the table for the most part. The exception might be verbal commands for one's dog-like "sit" and "speak." If you happen to have a parrot, the language will have a presence. These exceptions notwithstanding, you can explore the aspects of communication that are not linguistic, such as tones and gestures. Think about how you control the way you communicate with others through every facet of your being.

A fourth activity is trying to understand what kind of interaction a pet wants and/or requires from its human owner. The benefit of this activity is explicitly examining the individuality of one's pet. This discursive activity is meant to allow you to wonder what your particular pet wants and expects from you.

Once you've thought about all of the things this very different kind of being wants and needs from you, think about how important you are to the different kinds of beings in your life. Think about how much you do for the people in your life. Think about how much effort you put into giving others what they want or expect from you.

Think about how much control you have over that fact. Think about why you do these things for your pet or other people. Think about how it is your choice whether or not you do things for others. Think about your amount of control in various situations coming to mind.

A fifth activity is giving your pet what you have determined your pet wants and needs. This seems obvious, but the added thrust of this activity is the acknowledgment that you are choosing to do something for another being. This is not a one-time activity.

This activity should continue throughout the life of your pet. Each time something involving the treatment of one's pet comes up, you can return the thought that you are choosing to do something for your pet because your pet needs or wants something. Acknowledge the control you have over what you do for others.

A sixth activity is considering your pet's quality of life. A number of the previous activities mentioned might bring you to a discussion of what is meant by quality of life. It is good to consider what kind of life is worth living. This is a tricky question for humans to answer, but pets provide some insight into the basic needs of any animal, including humans. You should consider what would improve upon your pet's quality of life.

This will lead you to consider what qualities you expect and anticipate in their own lives. To what extent does your quality of life involve control over certain aspects of your life? To what extent did you lose control in your relationship with a narcissist? What in particular do you need to get back? How would it improve your quality of life to get it back?

Once you have identified these particular examples of things you no longer have control of that you would like to regain control over, you can adjust these activities to feel that sense of control. In the meantime, if you are still working to figure out what exactly you need, try the following activities. They will give you the feeling of control along with the acceptance of that which you truly have no control over, regardless of who you are in a relationship with.

Gardening

Gardening, like pets and walks, inspires questions about nature. Why do certain plants thrive in certain kinds of soil? What determines the color of a flower? Why aren't our tomatoes as big as the tomatoes at the grocery store? Gardening is a way to learn about nature, be humbled by nature, and interact with nature.

One activity is playing with potting soil. Children must dig in the dirt. Experience sand, wood chips, or whatever the playground provides. It is good to learn the difference between one type of ground and another. You might discover fascinating things about the difference between types of soil and why certain plants thrive in one type of soil, but not another.

Consider that when you were in a relationship with a narcissist, it was like you were planted in the wrong kind of soil. You could not grow there. The environment was not right. You were not getting the proper nutrients. The narcissist was like a weed, taking from you without sharing anything or giving anything back.

A second activity is to look for seeds and consider what kinds of plants grow best in your location. Again, compare your situation to the importance of certain conditions for certain plants to grow. Acknowledge that no matter how much potential a seed has, it will not grow in certain weather conditions. Your relationship with a narcissist was like being a seed planted in a place with the wrong weather conditions. You just couldn't reach your potential while you were there.

A third activity is, of course, planting. Touch the soil. Learn how to plant something. Label what you have planted. Share your plant's progress with others. Be proud of what you have done. Remember that you control everything about your plant that is within your control. You control its placement, soil, water, and anything else you have decided to take upon yourself. You can't control the weather, but you can control where your plant goes. You will learn how much of your environment is under your control once you plant things.

A fourth activity is measuring growth. It is incredible to watch things evolve. You can indulge yourself in bearing witness to evolution (change over time, not Darwin's theory) by recording the growth of your plant. Observe the difference day-to-day and week-to-week. Measure height, count leaves, takes notes, and acknowledges your part in its growth. You controlled so much of its potential to become anything more than a seed.

A fifth activity is pulling weeds. The concept of weeds as a metaphor for has already been somewhat introduced. The comparison was between the narcissistic abuse you experienced and the weed's activity of taking nutrients from other plants.

With that comparison standing, pull the weeds from your yard so that the plants you want to grow do not suffer the abuse of the weeds. Each time you pull a weed, consider that you're removing the narcissistic plants from your garden so that your plants can grow peacefully.

A sixth activity is growing particular herbs and learning the healing aspect of certain herbs. Marvel at the uses of different herbs. Consider whether or not, everything we need in this world to heal ourselves can be grown if we only utilize the resources at our disposal.

You might even discover some herbs that may help you relax. Relaxation will help with your recovery. You may also find herbs that heal your body, which will also be an aid toward your emotional recovery. The body and the mind are both better when each is well.

A seventh activity is observing insects. Get down and dirty with your garden. Pick up the earthworms. Release ladybugs into your rose bushes. Play with pillbugs, aka rollie pollies. Feel like the ruler of your domain. Find your power and be gentle with it. Don't be a narcissist, but find control over things that matter to you. Find control in your gentle nature.

An eighth activity is observing roots. Whether you're planting root vegetables like potatoes or pulling weeds, roots are fascinating things to examine. Play with the word *rootedness*. Look at it with a magnifying glass. Think about what root is and consider the importance of it in the garden and life. Remember that your roots are more important than whatever the narcissist you were with added to your branches.

A ninth activity is cleaning up. Gardening is a messy activity, but the organization is the key. Make sure you take on the activity of keeping a clean look to your garden. Your organized lines in the garden will give you a sense of order in life. Think about the correlation between aesthetics and useful boundaries. The narcissist in your life probably understood aesthetics, but not boundaries. You, on the other hand, actively make aesthetically pleasing boundaries in your garden with the knowledge that both are good.

A tenth activity is using gardening tools. Using tools will help you feel in control. Learning to wield a gardening tool is as (or more) useful as wielding any kind of tool one can think of. If you can control the objects in your hands, you can control the thoughts in your mind.

Perhaps gardening and taking care of your pet is not entirely sufficient for you to be sure you have regained all control you have lost, but it is certainly a start. Think about all of the things you do have control over. You haven't lost control. The narcissist you were with only made you think you had. You have it. Activities like caring for a pet and tending to your garden will remind you how much control you still have.

Practice these things often. If these activities don't appeal to you, find something that accomplishes the same tasks. Find another way to use tools. Find another way to see how much of your life is in your hands.

In the following chapter, there will be more attention focused on the particular practice of affirmation. You will be asked to practice affirming things, such as your control. You lost out on a lot of affirmation in your relationship with a narcissist. Since you are the root of your recovery, it is up to you to start affirming yourself.

Affirmation is the nutrition that the narcissist took from you. It is time for you to allow yourself to keep that nutritious goodness you became so good to making for a narcissist. You know you are good at affirming.

Your affirmations were what were asked of you from the narcissist you were with. It's time for you to turn those affirmations away from that person and toward yourself.

Chapter 7: Practicing Daily Affirmation

You must undo the negative thinking habits that you developed in your relationship with a narcissist. The best way to undo these habits is by replacing them with positive thinking. Find a way to be proud of yourself for what you have learned instead of upset with yourself for not knowing beforehand. There is nothing wrong with learning. From this experience, you have learned so much!

Think about your experience like a vaccination. Those who have yet to experience what you have experienced are more susceptible to falling ill than you are. Getting down on yourself for having had the experience will do you no favors, nor will deny your experience.

You must understand your experience the best you can and accept your part in the matter. Once you have done that, there is no point in begrudging yourself for the part you played. The only productive next step is to move forward.

The way to move forward is with daily activities and daily affirmations that will undo your negative sense of self. Hopefully, you have read the previous chapters on activities and are ready to get some ideas about daily affirmation.

The following reading is not comprehensive. It is only the start. You can find more affirmation readily available on the world wide web. The point of this chapter is to get you warmed up to the idea of receiving daily affirmation from yourself and acknowledging its importance to your recovery.

You Are Good Enough

Everyone is their own starting block. If you're reading this book, you like to turn to resources that help you tease out the intellectual secrets to life. You must believe that there is hope for you to feel better than you do right now. This is true.

Yet, this does not mean you are not already good enough. The fact that you are reading this book means you are better off than a lot of people who do not believe in their own ability to improve and recover. You obviously believe in yourself and want to feel better. That means you are good enough already.

Tell yourself that you are good enough to take the next step. You are always kind enough to take the next level. There is never a point where thinking you are too far behind will lead you to the next step.

You must understand that the only way to take the next step is to know that you are exactly where you need to be to take it. And, the truth is, you are. You are where you need to be to take the next step, always. That's the beauty of steps. You are right where you need to be to move forward. It's only a matter of doing so.

You Deserve to be Happy

Tell yourself that you deserve to be happy. Why? Well, for one thing, if you were in a relationship with a narcissist, you might not have thought about your happiness for quite some time. You were more concerned with someone else's happiness, weren't you? You put the happiness of others before yourself. Good for you. You're not a narcissist. BUT you deserve to be happy, too.

Start to think of yourself as some others would. Think about how you would go about making yourself happy if you were someone else. Then, go about doing it. Think about what makes you happy. Tell yourself that there is nothing wrong with making yourself happy in the same way you make others happy.

I trust that you don't go around making others happy by hurting other people. The same rule applies to make yourself comfortable. If you can make yourself happy without hurting anyone else or creating negative consequences for yourself, there is no reason not to make yourself happy in the healthy, appropriate way in which you have been making others happy for a long time. It's your turn. You deserve it.

It is Okay to Feel Shame Sometimes

Unlike the narcissist you were with, you know the feeling of shame pretty well. You know it because the narcissist you were with made you take on their shame. This was very generous of you. This shows that you have empathic abilities the narcissist does not possess. Yet, you took on a lot of shame that wasn't your own. This is not the appropriate way to feel shame. Your shame should be your own.

The narcissist saw you as an extension of his or her self because that's how narcissists approach the world, and they passed their shame onto you because they could not feel it in themselves. It is time for you to reclaim your shame. Feel shame; that's fine.

Don't overcompensate by taking up the narcissists tricks to avoid shame. Make that shame your own. If you feel ashamed of something, ask yourself if the shame you feel is your own or someone else's. If it's your own, good! Feel it, and then move on. That's all there is to it. Be proud of the fact that you can feel for yourself again, regardless of whether or not the feelings are good or bad.

Check in to see what you're feeling. Don't avoid all bad feelings. You won't recover in avoidance. Do give yourself credit for feeling your feelings, though! This is the pathway to your recovery. Feel things, but ask yourself whose feelings you're feeling. It may have been a while since you were sure you were feeling for yourself and not for them. Be proud of yourself for every feeling that you know to be your very own!

Love Yourself for Loving Others (Even Narcissists)

Do not get down on yourself for loving someone who turned out not to be the person you thought they were. Do not get down on yourself for loving anyone. Be proud of yourself for having the capacity to love.

Be proud of yourself for putting so much of yourself into that relationship. Be proud of it, accept the reality of it, and then move forward and look for something new.

The appropriate response to loving someone that turned out to be bad for you is to try to find someone to love that will be good for you. Now, you have a better idea of what is bad for you. That's an excellent thing. Love yourself for loving them, even if you decided in the end that it was too draining.

Enjoy the fact that you are full of so much love that you could be with a narcissist, but then take steps to be with someone who can give that kind of love back to you. It is so good that you are capable of loving. You deserve to be loved back by someone else who is just as capable.

Be Proud of What You Learned from Your Experience

There is nothing helpful about thinking negatively about you because of this experience. You will only gain from positive thinking about your experience. Think about what you have learned. Be glad for that. Imagine you had not learned it yet, and you were about to fall victim to the love of a narcissist next week! It is good that you learned what you learned.

Tell yourself this every time you start to think negatively about what you went through. Tell yourself that regardless of the pain caused by the narcissist, it is good that you learned enough to avoid suffering the same pain again in the future.

Be Proud of Who You Have Become

Think about who you were when you met the narcissist you were with a relationship. Are you different now? How so? Instead of beating up on who you were, be proud of you are now! Think about who you have become, in addition to what you have learned. Tell yourself that you are glad you have changed the way you did. Find ways to complement yourself for being who you are today.

Stop coming up with reasons to blame yourself for actions taken in the past. Start coming up with reasons to compliment yourself for the actions you are taking right now.

Be Proud of Your Boundaries

You have boundaries. They were violated for a long time. Think positively about the boundaries you set for yourself. Acknowledge them every day. Own them. The narcissist you were in a relationship probably neither respected nor understood your boundaries. This might mean you need to protect your boundaries with extra force right now. Maintain them as needed, but the most important thing is that you respect yourself for having them.

You simply need to respect yourself for having them the way the narcissist did not respect you for having them. You should also understand them better than the narcissist could. Maintaining them may or may not always be a possibility. Boundaries are violated all the time. People do not always understand the boundaries of others. You cannot control these facts.

You can, however, control the way you feel about your own boundaries. The worst offense of the narcissist you were in a relationship was not violating your boundaries. They didn't know any better because they didn't understand your boundaries. The worst offense by them is that they made you feel negative about your boundaries. What you can control at this point is how you feel about your boundaries. You can decide which of your boundaries is worth maintaining and, in general, whether or not you feel good or bad about your boundaries. The point is to make up your own mind about the value of your boundaries. You no longer have to evaluate their merit by the standards of a narcissist who cares little for them.

Be Proud of Your Ability to Feel Shame

There have been some intentional repetition on this particular aspect of recovery because it is more complicated than affirming oneself, but the two things are not necessarily desperate. You can allow yourself to feel shame and accept the reality of your situation without thinking negatively about yourself or your situation. Once you have allowed yourself to feel shame, be proud of yourself for feeling it. Then, allow yourself to move on from it and respond appropriately.

Take the next step to feel better within the scope of reality. The narcissist you were with liked to take the easy way out of shame by imagining a new narrative. Love the narrative you know to be true, even if it involves feelings like shame. Shame is part of the human narrative, but you can feel good about yourself for being able to feel shame and overcome it without escaping from it through fantasy and denial.

Be Proud of Your Desire to Know Reality Over Fantasy

Seeking fact over fiction separates you from the narcissist you were with. You've endured the emotional abuse of their manipulation of your reality. Now, you get to choose reality and think positively about it. The narcissist you were with made you feel your fact seeking was negative (when the narcissist turned out to be wrong about something), but now you get to return to your love of reality. Be proud of the things they made you feel bad about.

Love the fact that you love the facts. Recall all of the times that they had an outburst because you simply corrected them with the facts. Appreciate the fact that you did that. It is not a bad thing that you want to know the truth. Unfortunately, the narcissist you were with could not handle the truth when it was against them.

Be Proud of Who You Are
This is pretty close to being proud of who you have become, but as you get closer to changing your negative thinking to positive thinking, you should be thinking less about the past.

The difference between being proud of who you have become and what you learned from the experience is simply being proud of who you are in the absence of having to look back upon the relationship you had with a narcissist.

Eventually, you will want your daily affirmations to move completely away from having anything to do with the relationship you were previously in. You must start by directly affirming yourself in the ways the narcissist denied you, but the next step will be affirming yourself without even thinking about the narcissist you were in a relationship with.

You Deserve to Recover

It is important that along your way to recovery, you are always reminding yourself that you deserve your recovery. Negative thinking about your recovery could cause a setback. You must remain positive about your recovery, no matter what. Be patient with yourself. Believe that you deserve your recovery. Be proud of the steps you have taken. Be proud of what you have accomplished.

Do not think about what you have yet to accomplish except for setting your sights on the next step you wish to take. Maintain a positive attitude toward that step.

Remain positive about yourself even though you still have steps ahead of you.

Tell yourself every day that you deserve to recover from narcissistic abuse. Do not get stuck criticizing yourself for needing to recover. Stay focused on the hope that you will recover and the fact that you ought to recover. You do deserve to recover. You deserve to recover because you're putting effort into recovering. That's the difference between the entitlement of a narcissist and a healthy desire for a well-deserved recovery.

As long as you're putting in an effort, you deserve your recovery. Remind yourself that you are not simply entitled to recovery but that you are working toward your recovery.

Therefore, you deserve it because you are putting effort into it. You are setting an effort in because you deserve it. In the end, all that matters is that you are working toward the recovery you deserve. That's all there is to it.

You Deserve a Better Relationship

Lastly, you deserve a better relationship next time. Whether you are actively seeking a new relationship, or wish to be single for some time, tell yourself that you deserve a better relationship. Perhaps you do not want a better relationship yet, but you should still tell yourself that you deserve a better one next time around. Think about what you want. Think about it, realistically. Think about what you can contribute to a relationship. Think about reasonable expectations you might have of your next partner.

Tell yourself every day that you deserve a better relationship with yourself and with your next romantic partner. Do not get stuck criticizing yourself for the relationship you had before. Stay focused on the hope that your next relationship will be different and the fact that you ought to have a different kind of relationship the next time around.

Chapter 8: Allowing Yourself to Be Who You Are

The last part of your road to recovery is allowing yourself to be who you are. Who you are is a combination of you were before, are right now, and where you would like to be in the future. Who you were when you were in a relationship with a narcissist might feel distant from you now, but this experience is part of you now.

You might not have felt like yourself for a while, but you have always been you. Now it is time for you to be comfortable with who you are.

Therein lies the main difference between who you were then, and you want to become. You want to become comfortable with yourself again, right? That's the final goal for your recovery.

If you are still unsure how to do that, do not fret. This chapter has recommendations for this completion of your recovery. There are a lot of ways to become comfortable with who you are. The activities from previous chapters are sure to have helped you do this already.

The following activities are geared to maintain the progress of your recovery. If the previous activities helped you reclaim your identity, the following activities would help you maintain a level of comfort with the identity you have begun to establish.

Separate Your Identity from the Narcissist

You must separate your identity from the narcissist. Do not try to continue running in the same circles as the narcissist. Find new friends. Keep your work life and social life as separate from the narcissist as possible. You might have family ties, divorce, or custody considerations about this. Of course, there may be circumstances that simply do not allow for your separation.

Yet, you must separate in the ways you can. You will need to ask yourself if your identity is still bound to the narcissist in any way. Perhaps the answer is yes, but the connection is unavoidable. That's fine. You'll simply have to do your best with your internal recognition of yourself. If the answer is yes and you know that it is in your control and that you could change things, then you need to make a change.

You need to be comfortable with your separate identity. You need to have things that you do that are your own. You need to make friends that have never even met the narcissist. You need to feel like who you are now is different from who you were then, even if who you back then remained part of you. There are parts of yourself that must always be kept.

The point of this message is that you need to keep adding to your identity. The important aspect of these new additions regarding your recovery is that these new additions separate you from the narcissist. They should not pull you backward. They should push you forward.

Find Something That Makes You Feel Strong

This is an ambiguous heading, but it is meant to work both figuratively and literally. In other words, you could read this as a suggestion to hit the gym if you would like. You could also read this as an incentive to join a support group of some sort. Either works.

The point is to find something that makes you feel strong in whatever sense you would like to feel stronger. If you want to gain mental toughness, you ought to take a class that involves something you're afraid. Challenging yourself to do something that scares you builds mental toughness.

If you would like to feel physically stronger, you should find a way to accomplish this. You could get Pilates DVDs or a personal trainer. What feels right for you is what is right for you. Perhaps you enjoyed the simple yoga poses recommended in a previous chapter, and you would like to pursue yoga further.

The point is that you pursue some activity that will make you stronger, and therefore, make you feel confident. Strength will help you maintain your recovery. Strength will keep you motivated. Strength will keep you from relapsing. Find some activity that you pursue for a length of time that will make you stronger in whatever way you deem valuable.

Be Extremely Honest and Upfront

A lot what was hurtful about the relationship you were in with a narcissist is that a lot of it was a lie. This person turned out to be something other than you thought they were. This person turned out not to care about you the way you thought they did. This person turned out to be able to hurt you in a way you never expected of them. It is, therefore, important that you become more honest than you have ever been. This will help you maintain your sense of self. It will also help you avoid dishonesty in your next relationship.

The next time you meet someone you find interesting, be as upfront and honest with them as you can be. See what their reaction was like. The narcissist you were with was probably not a huge fan of honesty, at least not when it came to anything negative about them. You may have avoided honesty for a long time because of this. You don't have to anymore. You should do things a little differently from now on. Be as honest as you want to be.

Be as honest as you want someone to be with you. Be upfront about what you are looking for. Be upfront about who you are. You are angered at the fact that the narcissist you were with hid their true selves from you. Don't hide your true self from the people you meet. Be the person you want to be and be honest about who that person is. Undo the cognitive dissonance exercised by the narcissist in which the image of a person matters more than the actual person. Be more than an image. Be honest. Be real. Be you.

Be Assertive

If you've managed to be honest and upfront, you can manage to be assertive. The difference is simply the confidence behind your honesty. Assertive means you're self-assured. Being assertive means you have been honest with yourself, and you know what you think about something.

Then, once you know what you honestly think, you express yourself as someone who knows exactly what they think is the truth. That's being assertive. You can't really be assertive until you've learned how to be honest with yourself and others.

An assertive person has undeniable confidence because they aren't at odds with themselves. They know what they're saying. They believe they're right to say it.

Be assertive. Be someone who reflects on what they want and is not afraid to ask for it because they are certain their request is within reason. This is different from being entitled to the way a narcissist is entitled. Entitlement means you expect to get things without having to work for them. Being assertive means being willing to ask for something because you *know* you deserve them, and you are confident that anyone else should be able to see this.

The big difference is that you should know you deserve what you have asked for. A narcissist often thinks they have been wronged in some way because they don't already have what they deserve. Someone assertive knows that they don't just get to have things, but they are willing to stand up for themselves when they know that they have been cheated.

Be Outgoing

Part of establishing yourself and being you has to be done in front of and with others. There are a lot of ways in which your recovery can take place in isolation, but at some point, you need to go out and meet new people who can observe you as you are right now. The narcissist you were with was probably jealous when you were particularly outgoing and attracted more attention than they did. You may have held yourself back for their sake. It's time to be outgoing again.

They are no longer an excuse to hold you back. Get out there and get attention. There is nothing wrong with getting attention or with liking attention. The narcissist probably made you feel ashamed if you took care away from them, but they cannot shame you anymore.

Be outgoing and perhaps even flirtatious. You will feel better once you find yourself able to go out and feel attractive again without worrying that you're hurting the narcissist's feelings. The point is not to become the town spectacle, but a little bit of fun will be good for you.

A little bit of attention will be healthy for you. A little bit of flirting will be just fine. Enjoy yourself. Make yourself enjoy being outgoing in a way you have not in however long it has been.

Try New Things

Part of the abuse of being with a narcissist is the feeling of being stuck. Narcissists get stuck easily because of their entitlement and their avoidance of reality. Trying new things will keep you from feeling stuck again. You might need to try a lot of new things at first. Eventually, you'll have recovered enough to settle back into a routine of some kind.

Until then, you might want to try something new daily, weekly, or as needed. Basically, any time you feel stuck in a way that reminds you of how you felt when you were with a narcissist, you should go out and try something new.
You will find that trying new things invigorates you. This is because it is, in many ways, an antidote for what you have been through. Narcissists can be very exciting and stimulation seeking, but they can also be a hindrance to their partner if they feel threatened by their partner trying new things.

In any case, trying new things will help you maintain your sense of identity. We learn new things about ourselves when we try new things. Anytime you feel the need to learn something about yourself, simply try something new. It will always do the trick.

Do Volunteer Work

Volunteer work is an incredible way to learn about yourself and feel good about yourself while stepping away from yourself. You step away from yourself when you volunteer because you are doing something for someone else.

You might think this kind of work would be counterproductive because you have been volunteering your efforts to the narcissist for so long, but it will actually feel good to place the same kind of efforts elsewhere.

You must distribute your efforts between yourself and others still. You don't want to become like a narcissist. You just need to make up for your lack of self-love.

Combine your self-love and other-love now. The problem with being with a narcissist is that your love was going into a leaky vessel. You kept giving it, and it was received, but it never filled either of you up. The reason for this is the leak. A narcissist's capacity for love is kind of like a leaky vessel because it is really hard to feel before it gets emptied again. You worked hard, but it didn't always yield the same result. Sometimes you were appreciated.

Narcissists know a little about positive reinforcement. Other times, you were not so successful. Volunteer work should be more fulfilling work than the work you did for the narcissist. Sure, it may never feel as good as it felt those few glorious times when the narcissist gave you the recognition you deserved, and it's true.

A narcissist can make you feel really good about the work you did for them. There's no denial about that to be found in this book. Still, since the narcissist struggled enough to appreciate you that you have diagnosed them as a narcissist, then volunteer work will be a more reliable source of fulfillment than the narcissist was in your relationship.

Be Humble, but Don't Minimize Your Accomplishments

Being humble is tied to honesty and reality. You need to stay humble in order to maintain the success of your recovery. Getting too proud or boastful will not do you any favors. Be honest with yourself about your mistakes. Be honest with yourself about your successes.

It is likely that in your relationship with a narcissist, you were excessively hard on yourself for your mistakes, and you minimized your successes. Now you do not have to do either of those things anymore.

You may acknowledge your mistakes without feeling an abundance of shame. Feel a realistic amount and then move forward. Acknowledge that the amount of shame the narcissist you were with made you feel for a mistake was outrageous. Feel the amount of shame you think someone else should feel for that mistake and then move on to the next thing you have to do.

Don't minimize your accomplishments, either. Allow yourself an amount of celebration that you would deem appropriate for someone else. Think about what amount of celebration you think an accomplishment of that sort deserves and then grant yourself dessert of such a celebration.

Seek Counsel from Others

One thing that will really help you recover and maintain the status of your recovery is seeking counsel from others. A major hindrance one suffers from when in a relationship with a narcissist is the feeling that no one's opinion matters as much as the narcissist's opinion.

This is, of course, a myth the narcissist wanted you to believe. One way to stay far away from that fallacious line of thinking is to continuously seek counsel from others. Listen to a lot of other people. Listen to what all kinds of people have to say. Listen carefully. Listen well. Ask questions. Seek answers.

You must deny the myth of the narcissist every time you determine that another person's advice is worth listening to. This doesn't mean you have to do what other people tell you. The point is simply that you value what other people have to say as if all kinds of opinions matter. By accepting that all kinds of opinions matter, you make the opinion of the narcissist less special. That's what the narcissist wanted you to think—that their opinion of you was special. It is important that you consistently practice valuing the thoughts of others.

Making this, will help you recover from the feeling that the narcissist's opinion of you mattered more than anyone else's. It will also be good for you simply because it is a good way to live in this world. It is lonely to live in a world where few opinions, thoughts, and ideas matter.

Think about how much better it is to live in a world of so many thoughts, opinions, and ideas. The narcissist may have preferred a world in which everyone thought as they did, but you don't have to agree with that. At least not anymore.

Take Yourself to Dinner

It would be great for you to reward yourself for your work. If you think about what makes you stick with a fitness routine or a diet, the answer is probably the results or the reward. Reward yourself for your recovery. Take yourself out to dinner. Take yourself somewhere new and exciting.

Treat yourself to a little vacation. Reward yourself for taking steps toward your recovery. Think about how often you indulged the narcissist you were within rewarding themselves. Go ahead and give yourself a turn.

Taking yourself out to dinner is a sign of self-assurance. It takes confidence to go out to dinner simply because you feel you deserve it. You might not want to go alone. That's fine. Bring someone along. The point is that you reward yourself for doing good work. You deserve a palpable reward for your work. Sure, recovery is rewarding enough. Even so, you are more likely to maintain your recovery status if you are giving yourself positive affirmation for all of the work you have done to be right where you are.

Keep a Record of Your Work

Not only should you reward yourself, you should also keep a record of your work. This might even help you mark your success in a way that makes you more confident that you do, indeed deserve your reward. In other words, you can write down the activities you think would be helpful work for you.

Then, you can write down the kind of reward you think you deserve for the completion of each activity. Then, you will not be stuck questioning whether or not you deserve a reward for your work or not. You will already have decided what your rewards should be for certain work and certain activities.

It is important that you can see what you have done so that you can feel proud of your work and motivated to continue it. One benefit of having a personal trainer for fitness is having that trainer keep a record of your results. It is important for any regime that a record is kept. Otherwise, you will be unable to assess your progress.

Keep a record in some fashion. Keep a journal. Post the positive affirmations you maintain on social media. Whatever suits your style is the right way to record your work. The point is simply that you find some way to measure your progress so that you may appreciate it.

Remember, you deserve to appreciate your accomplishments. Don't minimize anything about yourself anymore. You don't have to worry about hurting someone else's feelings because you get attention for being who you are. Be who you are.

Be proud of yourself. Be honest about your accomplishments. This includes celebrating the ones worth celebrating.

Conclusion

Thank you for making it through to the end of *Narcissistic Abuse Recovery: How to Recover Emotionally from a Relationship with a Narcissist and Reclaim Your Identity*, let's hope it was informative and able to provide you with all of the tools you need to achieve your goals whatever they may be.

The next step is to practice regaining control and recover from your relationship with someone with Narcissistic Personality Disorder. Having read the first couple of chapters of this book, you have equipped yourself with knowledge of the basics of Narcissistic abuse, its causes, its signs, and symptoms, as well as its different forms.

Gaining this understanding has hopefully shown you that the abuse you have experienced was not your fault. The following chapters should have provided some much-needed affirmation of what you have been through and why you deserve the time to recover. Further, you should understand that you are not alone.

Anyone who has had a relationship with someone with Narcissistic Personality Disorder has experienced narcissistic abuse in some capacity. None of these explanations condone the abuse, but hopefully, it has helped you understand that what you can do to prompt your recovery and begin to treat yourself better than you were treated in your relationship.

Your path to recovery involves understanding, acknowledgment, affirmation, and perhaps therapy. This book should have explained the benefits therapy will have on your recovery process in addition to giving you plenty of tools to work with on your own. Good luck on your way to recovery. Remember that regaining control must be practiced until it becomes natural once again.

Finally, if you found this book useful in any way, a review on Amazon is always appreciated!

Made in the USA
Coppell, TX
25 April 2021